CONGRATULATIONS!

You've Just Passed Grade 2

ALTO SAXOPHONE

D1797308

Exclusive distributors:

International Music Publications Limited: Griffin House, 161 Hammersmith Road, London W6 8BS, England
International Music Publications Germany: Marstallstrasse 8, D-80539 München, Germany
Danmusik: Vognmagergade 7, DK-1120 Cioenhage K, Denmark
Nuova Carisch Srl.: Via Campania 12, San Giuliano Milanese, Milano, Italy
Carisch France, SARL: 20, rue de la Ville-l'Eveque, 75008 Paris, France
Nueva Carisch Espana S.L.: Via Magallenes 25, 28015 Madrid, Spain

Production: Miranda Steel

Music arranged and processed by Barnes Music Engraving Ltd
East Sussex TN22 4HA, England

Cover design by xheight design limited

Published 2000

IMP

International
MUSIC
Publications

International Music Publications Limited
Griffin House 161 Hammersmith Road London W6 8BS England

Flying Without Wings

Words and Music by Steve Mac and Wayne Hector

What Shall We Do With The Drunken Sailor?

Traditional

La Donna e Mobile
(from Rigoletto)

Music by Giuseppe Verdi

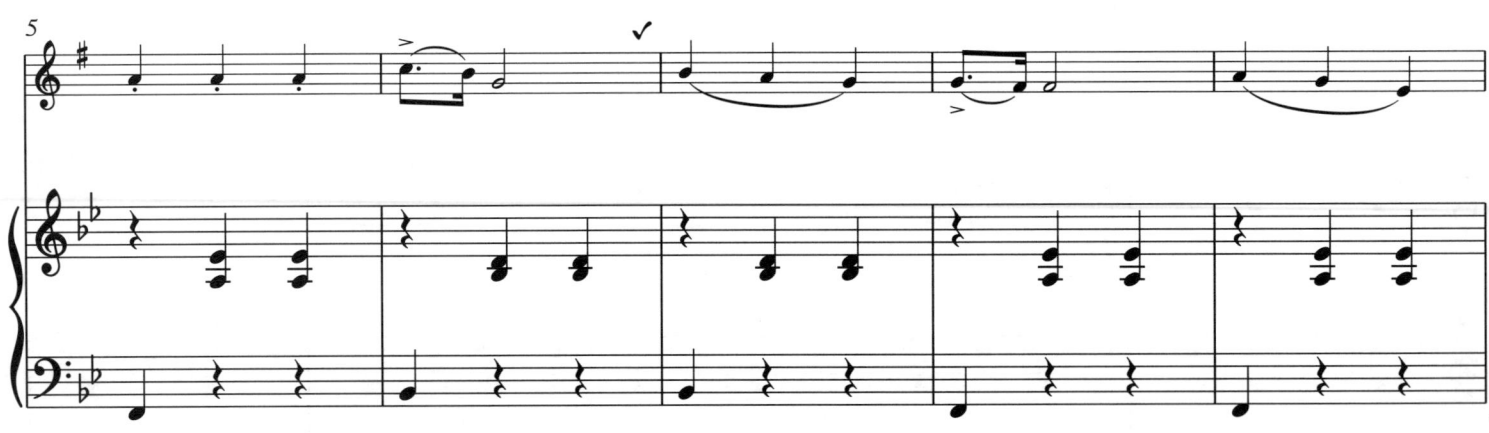

From The Heart

Words and Music by Diane Warren

CONGRATULATIONS!

You've Just Passed Grade **2**

ALTO SAXOPHONE

Flying Without Wings

Words and Music by Steve Mac and Wayne Hector

What Shall We Do With The Drunken Sailor?

Traditional

La Donna e Mobile
(from Rigoletto)

Music by Giuseppe Verdi

From The Heart

Words and Music by Diane Warren

As Long As He Needs Me

Words and Music by Lionel Bart

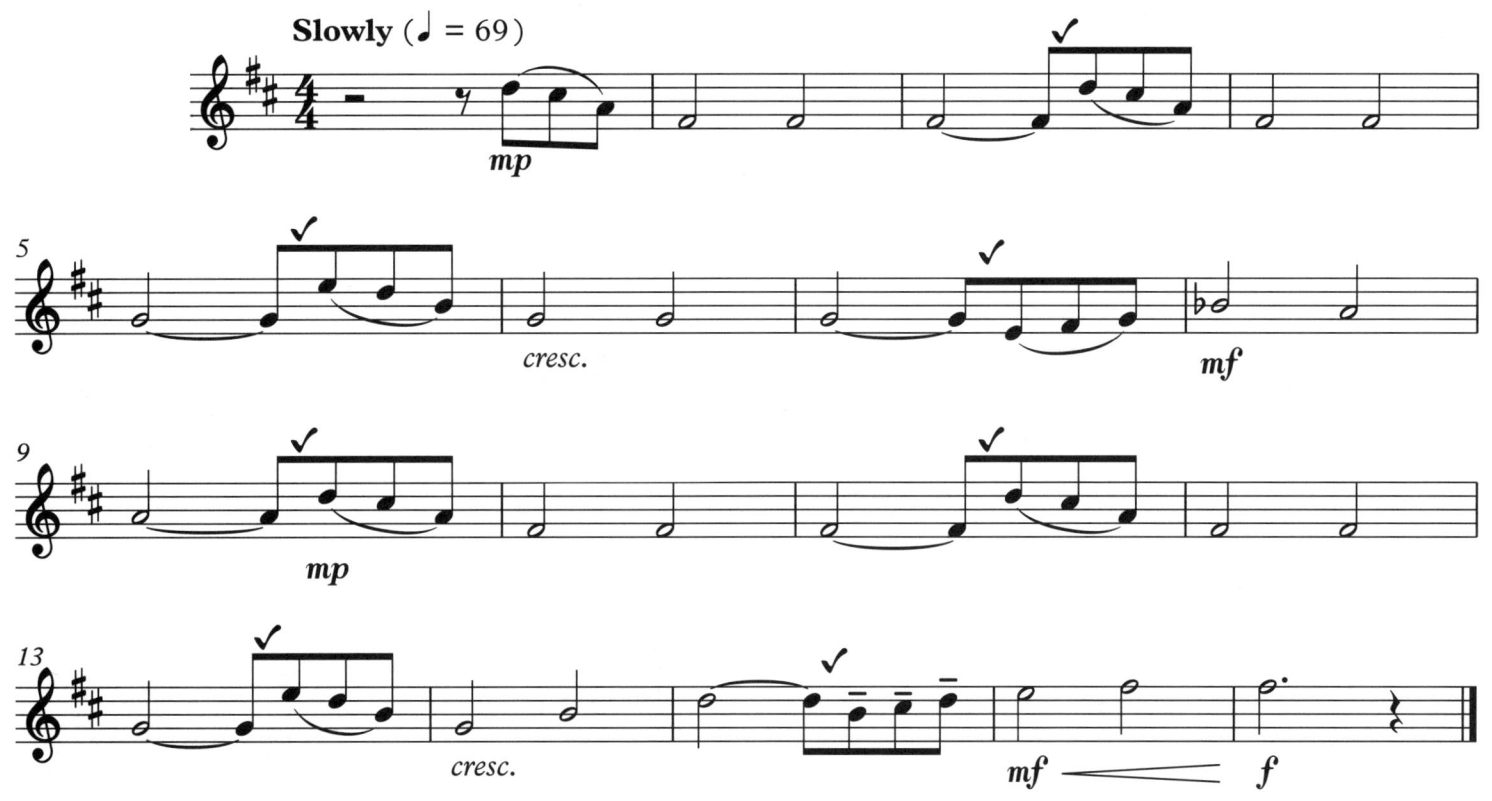

Sentimental Journey

Words and Music by Bud Green, Les Brown and Ben Homer

Autumn Leaves

Music by Joseph Kosma

Snowflakes

Words and Music by Arthur Jackson and George Gershwin

I'll Be There For You
(Theme from 'Friends')

Words and Music by David Crane, Marta Kauffman, Phil Solem, Danny Wilde and Allee Willis

Five Foot Two, Eyes Of Blue

Music by Ray Henderson

Cabaret

Music by John Kander

Frozen

Words and Music by Madonna Ciccone and Patrick Leonard

Black Bottom

Music by Ray Henderson

Summer Holiday

Words and Music by Bruce Welch and Brian Bennett

Blueberry Hill

Words and Music by Al Lewis, Larry Stock and Vincent Rose

Little Brown Jug

Traditional

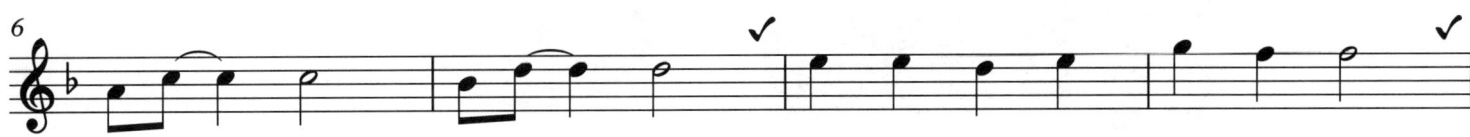

Printed by
Halstan & Co. Ltd., Amersham, Bucks., England

You can be the featured soloist with
TAKE THE LEAD

Collect these titles, each with demonstration and full backing tracks on CD.

90s Hits	Movie Hits	TV Themes	Christmas Songs	The Blues Brothers
The Air That I Breathe (Simply Red)	**Because You Loved Me** (Up Close And Personal)	**Coronation Street**	**The Christmas Song** **(Chestnuts Roasting On An** **Open Fire)**	**She Caught The Katy And** **Left Me A Mule To Ride**
Angels (Robbie Williams)	**Blue Monday** (The Wedding Singer)	**I'll Be There For You** (theme from *Friends*)	**Frosty The Snowman**	**Gimme Some Lovin'**
How Do I Live (LeAnn Rimes)	**(Everything I Do)** **I Do It For You** (Robin Hood: Prince Of Thieves)	**Match Of The Day**	**Have Yourself A Merry** **Little Christmas**	**Shake A Tail Feather**
I Don't Want To Miss A Thing (Aerosmith)	**I Don't Want To Miss A Thing** (Armageddon)	**(Meet) The Flintstones**	**Little Donkey**	**Everybody Needs Somebody** **To Love**
I'll Be There For You (The Rembrandts)	**I Will Always Love You** (The Bodyguard)	**Men Behaving Badly**	**Rudolph The Red-Nosed** **Reindeer**	**The Old Landmark**
My Heart Will Go On (Celine Dion)	**Star Wars (Main Title)** (Star Wars)	**Peak Practice**	**Santa Claus Is Comin'** **To Town**	**Think**
Something About The Way **You Look Tonight** (Elton John)	**The Wind Beneath My Wings** (Beaches)	**The Simpsons** **The X-Files**	**Sleigh Ride**	**Minnie The Moocher** **Sweet Home Chicago**
Frozen (Madonna)	**You Can Leave Your Hat On** (The Full Monty)		**Winter Wonderland**	
Order ref: 6725A – Flute	Order ref: 6908A – Flute	Order ref: 7003A – Flute	Order ref: 7022A – Flute	Order ref: 7079A - Flute
Order ref: 6726A – Clarinet	Order ref: 6909A – Clarinet	Order ref: 7004A – Clarinet	Order ref: 7023A – Clarinet	Order ref: 7080A - Clarinet
Order ref: 6727A – Alto Saxophone	Order ref: 6910A – Alto Saxophone	Order ref: 7005A – Alto Saxophone	Order ref: 7024A – Alto Saxophone	Order ref: 7081A - Alto Saxophone
Order ref: 6728A – Violin	Order ref: 6911A –Tenor Saxophone	Order ref: 7006A – Violin	Order ref: 7025A – Violin	Order ref: 7082A - Tenor Saxophone
	Order ref: 6912A – Violin		Order ref: 7026A – Piano	Order ref: 7083A - Trumpet
			Order ref: 7027A – Drums	Order ref: 7084A - Violin

As Long As He Needs Me

Words and Music by Lionel Bart

Sentimental Journey

Words and Music by Bud Green, Les Brown and Ben Homer

Autumn Leaves

Music by Joseph Kosma

Snowflakes

Words and Music by Arthur Jackson and George Gershwin

Quite lively (♩ = 76)

I'll Be There For You
(Theme from 'Friends')

Words and Music by David Crane, Marta Kauffman, Phil Solem, Danny Wilde and Allee Willis

Five Foot Two, Eyes Of Blue

Music by Ray Henderson

Cabaret

Music by John Kander

Frozen

Words and Music by Madonna Ciccone and Patrick Leonard

Black Bottom

Music by Ray Henderson

Summer Holiday

Words and Music by Bruce Welch and Brian Bennett

Blueberry Hill

Words and Music by Al Lewis, Larry Stock and Vincent Rose

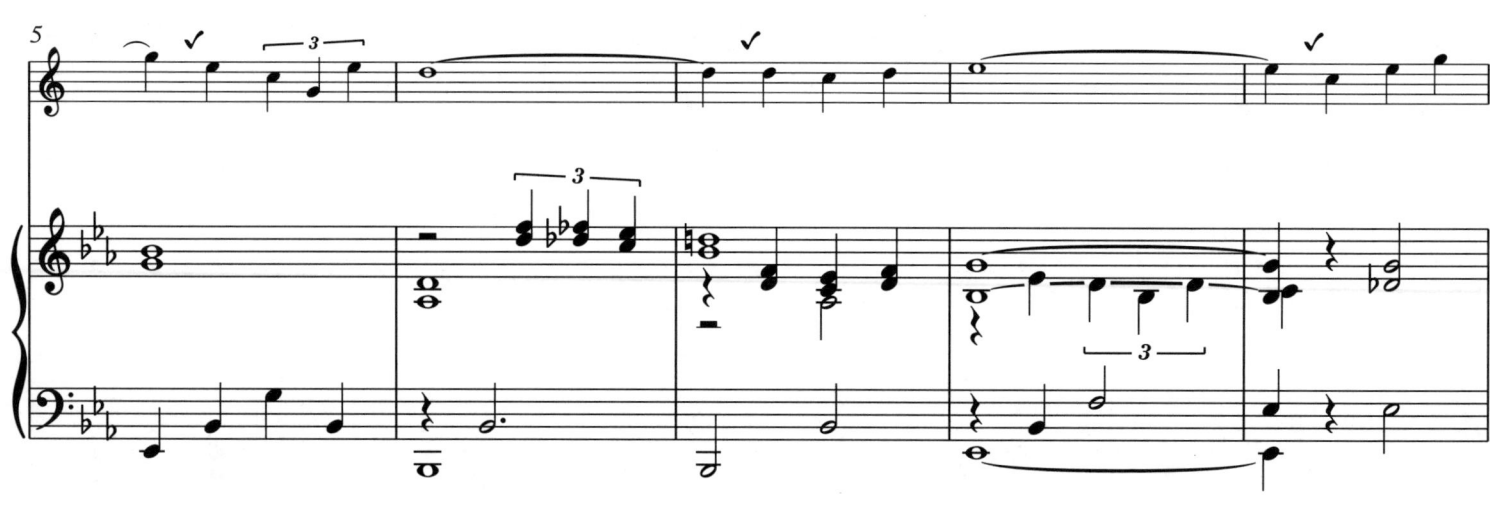

Little Brown Jug

Traditional

Printed by
Halstan & Co. Ltd., Amersham, Bucks., England

The Book contains the Head and first solo chorus of each piece written out in full so that you can play along. There are repeats of the chorus and space in the book so that you can write out your own solo ideas, plus we give harmonic and rhythmic ideas to help with your improvising. The Initial Level also gives scale choices to guide you to the notes on the solo sections. The accompanying text gives fascinating detail on the background to the pieces, along with practice tips, explanation of harmony and ideas for further listening.

The CD features professional jazz musicians. It gives audio reference to some of the text examples as well as a complete performance of each piece in demonstration and backing track versions. The demonstration track features solo improvisations by a professional player, giving you extra ideas for your own soloing. You can play along with this track to gain confidence and then launch into the backing track version to try out your own improvisations with the live rhythm section.

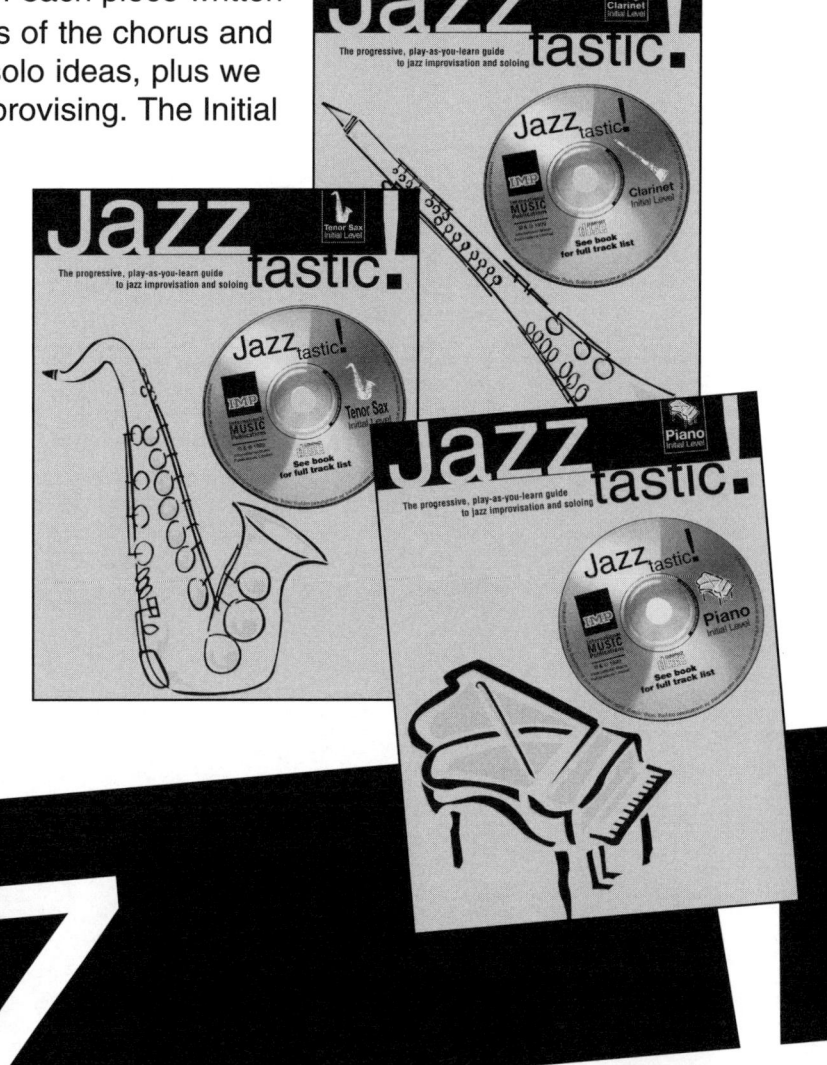

The progressive, play-as-you-learn series that goes the extra mile to give you everything you need to start improvising in authentic jazz style.

The Initial Level features these well-known jazz standards:

Basin Street Blues
C Jam Blues
Green Onions
Now's The Time
One O'Clock Jump
Peter Gunn Theme
Summertime
Watermelon Man

The Intermediate Level contains these jazz classics:

Don't Get Around Much Anymore
In A Mellow Tone
Jumpin' At The Woodside
Let There Be Love
Minnie The Moocher
Moondance
Stormy Weather
Sweet Home Chicago

Flute	**Order Ref:7060A**	Flute	**Order Ref:7070A**
Clarinet	**Order Ref:7061A**	Clarinet	**Order Ref:7071A**
Alto Saxophone	**Order Ref:7062A**	Alto Saxophone	**Order Ref:7072A**
Tenor Saxophone	**Order Ref:7063A**	Tenor Saxophone	**Order Ref:7073A**
Trumpet	**Order Ref:7064A**	Trumpet	**Order Ref:7074A**
Piano	**Order Ref:7065A**	Piano	**Order Ref:7075A**